Animals with Jobs

Rodeo Animals

Judith Janda Presnall

KIDHAVEN PRESS™

THOMSON

GALE

San Diego • Detroit • New York • San Francisco • Cleveland
New Haven, Conn. • Waterville, Maine • London • Munich

Dedication
To my husband, Lance, who happily accompanies me to rodeos
and shares my enthusiasm for new adventures.

Acknowledgment
In appreciation for answering questions and reading her manuscript,
the author thanks the following:

Bruce Hunt, Rodeo Coach at West Hills Community College, Coalinga, California,
and PRCA champion in calf roping, team roping, and steer wrestling.

Ron Wechsler, Rodeo Coach at Los Angeles Pierce College, Woodland
Hills, California, and PRCA champion in team roping.

© 2003 by KidHaven Press. KidHaven Press is an imprint of The Gale Group, Inc.,
a division of Thomson Learning, Inc.

KidHaven™ and Thomson Learning™ are trademarks used herein under license.

For more information, contact
KidHaven Press
27500 Drake Rd.
Farmington Hills, MI 48331-3535
Or you can visit our Internet site at http://www.gale.com

LIBRARY OF CONGRESS CATALOGING-IN-PUBLICATION DATA

Presnall, Judith Janda.
  Rodeo animals / by Judith Janda Presnall.
    p. cm.
Summary: Discusses the varieties, training, safety, work, and retirement
of rodeo animals, including horses, calves, steer, and goats.
Includes bibliographical references and index.
  ISBN 0-7377-2052-2 (hardback : alk. paper)
  1. Rodeo animals—Juvenile literature. 2. Rodeos—Juvenile
literature. [1. Rodeo animals. 2. Rodeos. 3. Working animals. 4.
Animals.] I. Title.
  GV1834.P74 2004
  791.8'4—dc21

                                                          003010181

Contents

Chapter One

What Is a Rodeo?

A rodeo is an event in which cowboys and cowgirls compete in roping and riding. In some contests, competitors on horses rope fleeing calves and steers. In others, bucking animals often triumph over their riders by flinging them to the dirt.

Rodeos evolved from the ranch chores that cowboys performed in their work. These Old West tasks included roping cattle for medical treatment and branding, breaking wild horses to the saddle, and rounding up steers. Initially, local cowboys challenged each other's skills in casual events. Later, groups of cowboys from neighboring ranches held informal contests to see who was better at performing everyday ranching tasks. The first organized "Cowboy Tournament" to charge admission took place on July 4, 1888, in Prescott, Arizona.

Ranch hands work together to rope a calf for branding. Today, roping calves is a popular rodeo event.

The Animals

Horses are a mainstay of rodeo events. The preferred horse of rodeo riders is the American quarter horse. It has the **agility** of the working ranch horse and the speed of a racehorse. Roping horses are between five and fifteen years old. A **gelding** is ideal for the average rider because it is more predictable than a mare or stallion.

Calves and steers are not trained for their jobs at the rodeo. However, they are "preconditioned" at each **arena**. This means that the day before the rodeo, the stock contractor runs the animals through the chute gate, across the length of the arena, and into a catch pen a half-dozen

The American Quarter Horse is renowned for its strength, speed, and beauty.

A cowboy races after his quarry in a timed roping event.

times. After working several rodeos, calves and steers become accustomed to their job and know what to do.

Roping calves are of similar size, weight, and breed. Calves and steers are limited to working only one year in the rodeo, before they become too big.

The modern rodeo features two types of competitions: timed events and **roughstock** events. In timed events, the contestant's goal is to score the fastest time in his or her event. Timed events include roping and tying contests, steer wrestling, and barrel racing. Roughstock involves riding bucking horses and bulls. Riders must endure the bumpy, rough ride for eight seconds, and they get points for style and difficulty.

Timed Events

One example of a timed event is **breakaway** roping, where a contestant ropes a fleeing calf while riding a horse. After the rider ropes the calf, the contestant stops the horse. As the calf continues running forward, the catch rope "breaks away" from the saddle. This action stops the time clock. The contestant whose rope breaks away the fastest wins.

Horses and riders work together to rope a calf, exhibiting coordination and training.

Another timed event involves cowboys and cowgirls whose skills are advanced. Tie-down roping involves a rider who chases and ropes a calf. The rider then **dismounts**, runs to the calf, and throws it on its side. After tying any three legs together, the roper raises his hands to signal he or she is done.

In team roping, two riders on different horses rope a steer together. One rider ropes the steer's horns, and the other rider ropes the steer's hind legs. This difficult contest requires teamwork between the two riders. Both must do their jobs or they will be disqualified. The clock stops when their two horses face each other with the steer in the middle held by a taut rope on each end.

Wrestling a Steer

Steer wrestling is rodeo's quickest contest and also a timed event. The world record is 2.4 seconds. This contest requires two mounted riders—a steer wrestler and a hazer—and a steer. The object is for the steer wrestler (also called a bulldogger) to stop a running steer and topple it to the ground as fast as possible. Bulldoggers must be stout, strong men since steers weigh 450 to 750 pounds.

As in roping events, the steer is given a head start out of the **chute**. The hazer rides alongside the steer guiding it in a straight path for the bulldogger. When the bulldogger's horse pulls even with the running steer, the cowboy drops from his horse and grabs the steer by the horns. The bulldogger digs his heels into the dirt to slow the steer down. After stopping the steer, the wrestler tips the steer

A cowboy wrestles a steer to the ground in rodeo's fastest event.

over by wrapping his arm around the right horn and pulling up while pushing down on the left horn. The clock stops when the steer is on its side with all four feet pointing in the same direction.

Barrel Racing

An additional timed event—barrel racing—is a contest for women only. A rider must gallop a horse at top speed around three steel drums (or barrels) set about ninety feet apart. The drums can be touched or moved, but if one is knocked over, the contestant receives a five-second penalty.

Roughstock Events—Wild, Bolting Animals

Roughstock events attract the most attention because riders are at high risk of injury. In order to remain in the contest, a competitor must ride the animal for eight seconds. During the ride, judges rate the style of animal and rider. The rider controls the style by using his boot **spurs** to obtain the most action. Roughstock events include saddle bronc riding, bareback riding, and bull riding.

Riders want an animal that is difficult to ride. Nine-time professional world champion bucking bronc and bull rider Ty Murray says, "The best horses know when it's show time. They come out of that chute wanting to rear up and rip you off their back."[1]

As in ranching tasks, the horse is the central animal in the rodeo. Horses have jobs in all rodeo events. For some events, such as roping and barrel racing, they must have extensive training.

Chapter Two

Horse and Rider: Train, Practice, and Compete

Most cowboys and cowgirls train their own horses for roping events. They form a true partnership and bonding that shows in competition. Riders spend months and years practicing the various techniques needed to win contests. Six days a week, for one to four hours each day, horse and rider work to perfect their timing.

Training readies the horse for competition, but conditioning prepares the horse for the physical rigors of the sport by developing its muscles and lung power. Some trainers give their horses a four-mile workout several times during the week. Horses also get a day off—usually the Monday after a rodeo.

It takes years of training to produce a horse that has perfected its skills. Competitors consider their horses as

Training a rodeo horse takes a lot of hard work and dedication.

partners in the contest. Bruce Hunt, a member of the Professional Rodeo Cowboys Association (PRCA) and college rodeo coach, states their significance:

> Professional rodeo cowboys and girls, who make a living winning money by roping, steer wrestling, or barrel racing, give much of the credit to the horses they compete on. They realize that they are only as good as the horses they ride, and a close bond is formed. The welfare and care of their horses comes before their own needs.[2]

A cowgirl shows the bond between her and her horse that grows from long hours of practice and care.

Training a Roping Horse

Tie-down roping depends on teamwork between the horse and its rider. The mounted rider must rope and tie a calf in the shortest possible time. Trainers begin with the basic groundwork of acquainting the horse with the workings of a catch rope and a jerk line. The catch rope is used to lasso the calf; one end is tied to the saddle horn.

The jerk line is used to cue the horse to back up a few steps.

The jerk line is a long, soft rope attached at one end to the horse's bridle bit with the other end tucked in the roper's belt. After roping the calf, the rider runs to the animal, allowing the jerk line to slide out of the belt. While tugging at the bit, the jerk line falls to the ground. This tug signals the horse to move back a few steps to tighten the rope around the calf.

During initial training, no calf is used. Instead, the rider gets off the horse and walks out to where a calf would be. He or she faces the horse and shakes the jerk line to get the horse to step back until the rope tightens. To further implant the idea of keeping a taut rope, the trainer may practice roping a "dummy" calf (a haystack or a wooden sawhorse) so the horse will learn to stand tight against the catch rope.

Controlled Speed

Other skills the horse and rider must learn are how to score and rate cattle. Scoring is the act of giving the fleeing animal a legal head start. Rating is putting the rider in a good position to throw and maintain an even speed behind the calf. After groundwork, the cowboy begins drills using slow calves confined in a pen and a breakaway rope. The cowboy trains his horse to stop as soon as he ropes the calf. Scoring and rating take about six months of practice.

But competition requires more than jerk lines, catch ropes, scoring, and rating. The competitor must also learn to tie the calf's legs snugly and quickly.

Roy Cooper was a five-time world champion calf roper in the 1980s. From the age of ten, he practiced roping and tying calves every day. Sometimes he tied as many as fifty calves in a single afternoon. After supper, Roy practiced tying a dummy calf that his father made for him. The dummy was a two-foot block of wood with three attached rubber hoses that represented the legs of a calf. Roy perfected his tying speed practicing on the dummy.

Tie-Down Roping: A Horse and Calf on the Job

In roping competitions, a mounted rider starts from an enclosure called a box. A box is a three-sided fenced area with the fourth side opening into the arena. The calf or steer to be roped occupies a chute next to the box. When the chute door opens, a person called a "pusher" gives the chute animal a forceful rear-end shove to ensure a rapid exit.

Depending on the length of the arena, the animal is given a five- to thirty-foot head start before the roper begins the chase. The horse runs after the calf. When the calf is roped around the neck, the horse stops. The rider dismounts, runs to the animal, flanks it, and ties its legs together. After giving a "done" hand signal, the rider remounts the horse, walks it forward to relax the catch rope, and waits six seconds to see if the calf remains tied. If the calf kicks free, the roper receives no time, which means he is out of the contest.

In a different roping contest, no tying is required— just exceptional accuracy.

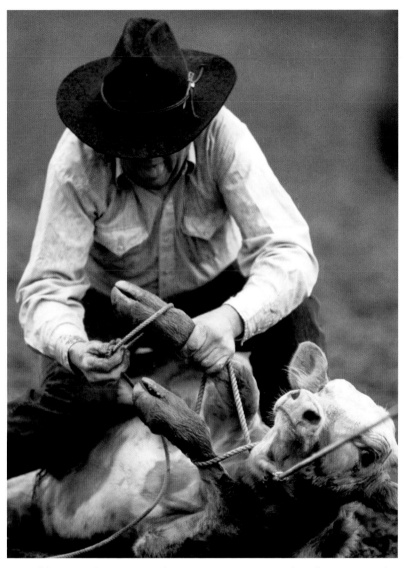

A calf struggles as a rodeo participant ties his legs securely.

Horses Train for Team Roping

Team roping involves two mounted riders working together to catch a running steer. One rider, called a
"header," loops the steer's horns; the other rider, called a

17

Steer roping takes a lot of practice, often without the animals used in competition.

"heeler," loops the steer's two hind legs. Header horses train for steer pulling by dragging a log with a rope that is tied to the horn on the saddle. This weight teaches the horse to keep a taut rope.

Header and heeler horses have different jobs. The header must score, rate, and wait for the catch. Then the header horse must turn sharply to the left and pull the steer to get it into position for the heeler. After the turn, the heeler can do his job. A heeler horse must stay behind the steer to allow the roper to get position to catch the steer's legs.

Both headers and heelers practice with their horses for many years—often from childhood—before they can compete. Leo Camarillo, four-time world champion team roper, sometimes roped as many as one hundred steers from his horse in a single practice day.

Teamwork

In rodeo competition, mounted header and heeler contestants begin in two separate boxes with the chute in the middle. When the steer dashes out of the chute and has its legal head start, the header horse catches up to the

Today's cowboys drive their horses to the rodeo in horse rigs made specially for the purpose.

running steer and then "rates" back to the same speed as the steer is traveling. When the steer is roped and turned, the heeler roper makes his throw at the hind legs. After this difficult catch, the horses must hold a taut rope with the steer in the middle to stop the clock.

Because rope horses need variety, some ropers own two trained horses. One horse may work rodeos for a couple of weeks and then go to the ranch for rest and time away from roping. The second horse is then available to take its place on the road. Competitors haul their horses thousands of miles on the rodeo circuit in trailers or custom-made **rigs**. Traveling can be as hard on horses' legs and bodies as the actual arena work.

Patience and persistence practiced during horse training pays off in the arena.

Chapter Three

Training for and Competing in Barrel Racing

In the 1950s, barrel racing was added to rodeos to allow women to compete. This event consists of a woman galloping a horse around three stationary barrels. This is done in a cloverleaf pattern, in which the rider makes a right turn around the first barrel, a left turn around the next, and a left turn around the third before rushing back to the starting line.

In barrel racing, the clock is the judge. Necessities are simple: three barrels, a woman, a horse, and the clock. The competition tests the horse's speed, balance, and agility as well as the competitor's riding and training ability.

A barrel rider and her horse work together to race around a barrel in a tight curve.

Training a Barrel Horse

Most women train their own horses. Training is best done in short time periods, due to a horse's short attention span. Although a riding session may last up to an hour, fifteen minutes of concentrated training during that time is enough. It takes up to two years for a woman to train her barrel horse.

At the first stage of practice, the trainer rides the horse at an easy gait, first in a large circle, then gradually in tighter circles with the horse's nose turned to the inside. Drills of figure eights, stops, and turns, make the horse flexible and limber in the shoulders. Barrel racing requires the rider to shift her weight, put pressure on the horse with her legs, and use the **reins** for turns.

Practice with barrels comes next. The rider will first walk, then jog, and finally **lope** the horse around cones set up around the barrel. The cones show the horse the "pocket" area—the space between horse and barrel. The horse must also learn to rate, or shorten its stride and prepare to turn. At the turning point, the rider, who has been standing in the stirrups, sits down in the saddle. The rider's weight cues the horse to get closer to the ground for tight turns.

In the beginning, a horse might be ridden around the barrels eight to ten times a day in a variety of patterns. A horse can sometimes be bored by this routine, so when it performs well in practice, it might be allowed to stop training early that day as a reward. The session ends with a gentle pat and rub, and loosening of the cinch, or strap, that secures the saddle. After unsaddling the horse, the rider may wash it off and tie it in the cool shade.

Keeping the Horse Interested in Training

Training must vary each day. Sharon Camarillo, a barrel racer who has qualified for four National Finals Rodeos (NFRs), says:

A cowgirl rewards her horse with a snack after a good day of training.

Barrel racing can become pretty dull for a horse. It's not like working a cow, or roping. There are three stationary [nonmoving] objects in the arena, and the horse can get sour [disagreeable] running the same pattern. In order to avoid this resentment, I've learned to do a lot of training and conditioning away from the barrels.[3]

Another way to avoid boredom is to take the horse to other arenas for practice. This is called seasoning. It helps the horse feel comfortable in new places. Six months of seasoning and trail rides offer a change of scenery.

Equipment for Horses

A horse must use protective equipment in barrel racing. Protective leg gear for horses includes bell boots and **splints** that protect the front legs and hooves from over-reaching, or overextending and striking a front foot while running. Overreaching also occurs when one front foot steps on the other in a turn. Horses also wear skid boots on their back legs to prevent burns when stopping hard and making tight turns. To keep from sliding in the saddle, cowgirls use a lightweight saddle that has a seat with front and back "fenders" made of rough leather, almost like sandpaper.

In Competition

With all the appropriate equipment and more than a year of training, the rider and horse are ready to test their expertise against competitors. By now, the horse instinctively knows the pocket area and hopefully can make close turns around the barrels.

In the contest, horse and rider burst into the arena at a full gallop crossing a tiny beam of light projected across the arena. This triggers an electronic eye, which starts the time clock. The rider, standing in her stirrups, directs her horse to the first barrel, where it quickly judges the pocket area and shortens its stride to turn. She now sits down in the saddle, and her weight cues the horse to bend deeply. They continue around two more barrels and head back out of the arena, again triggering the eye that stops the timer.

To protect their legs and hoofs, horses wear splints, bell boots, and skid boots.

A contestant can touch or move barrels. But if she knocks one over, a five-second penalty is added to her score time. Since time is measured in hundredths of seconds, a toppled barrel spells disaster for the barrel racer. The winning time for barrel racing ranges from fourteen to seventeen seconds, depending on the ground condition at the arena.

At the ten-day December 2002 NFR in Las Vegas, Nevada, champion barrel racer Charmayne James described the arena condition: "The ground at the Thomas & Mack [arena] was just as bad as we all expected it to be. The bottom gives way and slips right out from under you. Five girls hit barrels the first round."[4]

A Champion Barrel Racer

The best known and most successful barrel racing horse that ever lived is "Scamper," owned and ridden by Charmayne James. Charmayne had begun competing at the age of six in local contests. In 1984, Charmayne James became a World Champion Racer at the age of fourteen. She and Scamper continued to win the title for ten years in a row, through 1993. Scamper, an American quarter horse, was inducted into the Pro Rodeo Hall of Fame in Colorado Springs, Colorado, in 1996.

Scamper retired soon after his ten-year run of championships. But in 2002, Charmayne brought him to the NFR for **exhibition**. Charmayne recounts the experience:

Scamper stole the show today at the Sands Expo Center. The line of people waiting to get a picture of him was longer than the line wanting my autograph. . . . Everyone is amazed with Scamper, they all say "I can't believe he looks so great at 26."[5]

After not having won in nine years, Charmayne finally won her eleventh championship in 2002 at the NFR with her next horse, "Cruiser." Charmayne's winnings during that ten-day event tallied $66,582. However, it was in 1990, at age twenty, that Charmayne became the first million-dollar cowgirl!

Unlike the roping and barrel racing contests, the horses in the bucking events are untrained. In fact, the wilder they are, the better.

A barrel racer and her horse work as a team as they fly through the arena.

Chapter Four

Dangerous Events

In a rodeo, the most dramatic competitions are the events that involve an element of danger. Whether it is saddle bronc riding, bareback riding, or bull riding, all require the rider to have guts and determination. These "roughstock" events are dangerous because the aggressive, untrained animals can injure or even kill their riders.

Sources for Bucking Horses and Bulls

Rodeo bucking horses come from racetracks, ranches, and private owners who have deemed them unbreakable. Other horses are bred to buck. An example of a horse that came to the rodeo because he could not be broken is "Classic Velvet." Having failed as a team roping horse, the owners sold him to a California stock contractor. Classic Velvet found his niche in PRCA

Bucking animals often succeed in throwing their riders to the ground.

events, where he bucked bareback riders for seventeen years. He retired from the rodeo at age twenty-four.

Stock contractors provide the bucking animals, as well as steers and calves, at rodeos. More than seventy stock contractors operate ranches in the United States and Canada, where rodeo livestock rest in between rodeos.

Eight Seconds of Fury

In all three roughstock events, the rider must stay on his bucking animal for eight seconds while holding on with just one hand, or be disqualified. Each ride is worth one hundred points—fifty for the animal's bucking action and fifty for the rider's expertise in control and spurring. Special equipment provokes bucking action of horses and bulls.

Gear Used in High-Spirited Contests

Bucking animals do not like anyone on their back and instinctively try to fling them off. All the bucking animals brought to the rodeo are aggressive, and especially so when a rider sits on them. However, to encourage high kicking with their back feet, all horses and bulls wear a flank strap during the contest. This is a sheepskin-lined strip of leather placed around the animal's body between its last rib and the hip (like a belt around a person's waist). The tight flank strap boosts bucking instincts, and since the animal wears a flank strap only for bucking, it tells them to go to work. Cowboys also use blunt spurs to incite the animal and make it leap and bounce to get a good ride.

Other equipment is worn by roughstock competitors. To shield their bodies from injury, riders wear protective clothing such as a flak jacket (like a bulletproof vest) to protect their chest bones and organs; chaps, which are heavy leather trousers without a seat; and calfskin gloves. Some bull riders also wear a helmet and a catcher's mask to protect their head and face from wounds.

Saddle Bronc Riding

The object in saddle bronc competition is for the rider to stay on for eight seconds while demonstrating a smooth, effortless ride, in which his moves match the horse's moves.

Saddle bronc riding begins with the rider sitting on a horse in a chute behind a gate. Both of the rider's heels must be touching the horse above its shoulders. The feet must remain there until the horse's first jump out of the chute. When the rider nods, chute men tug open the huge gate.

Trying to unseat the rider, the bronc bucks, twists, turns, and leaps. The contestant cannot drop the thick rope rein or let his or her feet slip out of the stirrups. Dashing the boots—toes out—the rider spurs the horse. Some saddle broncs do not need much spurring to give fierce action.

The undisputed queen of saddle broncs is "Miss Klamath." This mare's perpendicular kick and the ability to kick higher on each jump made her practically unrideable. In her entire career, only once did a cowboy last on her back for eight seconds.

Bareback Riding

Most of the rules of saddle bronc riding apply to bareback riding, except no saddle and rein are used. Instead, the rider holds onto a "rigging," a leather strap with a suitcase-type handle on top. It is wrapped around the horse's rib cage. During the "jackhammer"

Cowboys wear leather chaps and vests to protect their bodies in riding competitions.

ride, the cowboy alternately bends his knees and straightens his legs dragging his spurs back and forth along the horse's neckline toward the rigging. But leaping, twisting, and bucking horses are not the only risky competitions.

Bull Riding: The Most Dangerous Sport

Bull riding is one of rodeo's most dangerous, volatile, and uncertain events. A rider tries to stay on a 1,500-pound thrashing animal while holding only a flat braided rope, which is looped around the bull's chest just behind the front legs.

A cowboy holds on tight to the single rope on a bucking bull and fights to stay on for 8 seconds.

The horned animal does not need to be spurred. It is already lively and will buck, jump, and spin in an effort to shake or toss off his rider. He may even try to twist his head to hook the cowboy with his horns. The more active the bull, the higher the score. Once a rider is bucked off, the most dangerous part of the sport is about to happen. He could be trampled, mutilated, or killed by the beast. The most famous tragedy of this kind happened in 1989 when a bull named "Taking Care of Business" trampled to death top rider Lane Frost in Cheyenne, Wyoming.

Bodacious

The most feared rodeo bull was Bodacious, born in 1988. By 1994, Bodacious had established himself as an ultra-fierce and lethal competitor. His famous technique of vertical leaps, forward lunges, and head snaps terrified all bull riders.

Over the span of his four-year career, he charged out of the chute with a rider aboard one hundred thirty-five times. Only eight times did a rider stay on his back for the required eight seconds.

Rodeo hand Phil Sumner says, "Some bulls intimidate some cowboys, but I've never seen a bull be able to in-timidate *all* the cowboys."[6]

Vicious Bodacious

Tuff Hedeman, the greatest and most famous rider on the **circuit**, actually was matched with Bodacious three times. In 1993, Hedeman stayed on and earned an out-standing ninety-five points. But at the 1995 Professional

Bull Riders World Championships, he was not so lucky. On the third jump, Bodacious threw his head back and smashed Hedeman in the face.

Hedeman walked out of the arena wearing a mask of blood. His smashed cheekbones, broken nose, missing teeth, and cracked jaw required twelve hours of surgery. Doctors reconstructed his face using six **titanium** plates.

Later that year at the NFR in Las Vegas, Nevada, Hedeman again was randomly assigned to ride Bodacious. Not wanting to risk his life, Hedeman briefly strad-

Rodeo animals work hard to provide entertainment for spectators.

dled Bodacious to remain eligible in remaining rounds. Then he let the bull leave the chute without him.

Bodacious bucked one more time at that NFR. He again crashed his huge head against the rider's face. Bo's owner Sammy Andrews retired him the next day. Andrews said, "If Hedeman turned him out, then everyone else would. We're not in the business to kill off bull riders."[7]

Retired at the peak of his career in 1995, Bodacious spent the rest of his life traveling to rodeos for exhibition and in his home pasture passing on his genes to future bucking stars.

Whether bull, steer, calf, or horse—all play an important role in the exciting sport of rodeo. The efforts of many people keep the animals in good performing health. This commitment makes the event enjoyable for all who attend rodeos.

Notes

Chapter One: What Is a Rodeo?
1. Quoted in Skip Hollandsworth, "The Greatest Cowboy Ever," *Reader's Digest*, March 2000, p. 74.

Chapter Two: Horse and Rider: Train, Practice, and Compete
2. Quoted from a written statement by Bruce Hunt, Rodeo Coach, April 8, 2003.

Chapter Three: Training for and Competing in Barrel Racing
3. Quoted in Sharon Camarillo, *Barrel Racing*. Colorado Springs, Colorado: Western Horseman, 1985, p. 6.
4. Charmayne James, "Charmayne James—From the NFR," Charmayne James Website, p. 1. www.charmaynejames.com.
5. Quoted in James, "Charmayne James," p. 1.

Chapter Four: Dangerous Events
6. Quated in *Gentlemen's Quarterly* (or *GQ*), September 1998, p. 292.
7. Quoted in Freeman Gregory, "Some Kinda Bull!" *Houston Livestock Show & Rodeo* magazine, August 1999. [www.hlsr.com/hmagazine/99aug/f-bull.html]

Glossary

agility: The ability to move quickly and easily.

arena: Area (indoors or outdoors) where the rodeo takes place.

breakaway: Something that separates easily when jerked.

chute: The small enclosure from which the calf, steer, or bull is released into the arena.

circuit: A regular route from one rodeo to the next rodeos.

dismounts: To get down from a horse.

exhibition: On display to the public.

gelding: A male horse that has been castrated, or had its testicles removed.

lope: To ride with a steady, easy gait.

reins: Two long, narrow leather straps attached to the bit of a bridle and used by a rider to control a horse.

rigs: A comfortable vehicle for traveling with horses.

roughstock: Rugged rodeo events that are judged on style rather than speed.

splints: Rigid devices used to prevent motion of a joint.

spurs: Spiked devices attached to a rider's boot heels and used to urge an animal to move quickly.

titanium: A strong, lightweight metal that will not wear away.

Organizations
to Contact

American Junior Rodeo Association (AJRA)
4501 Armstrong Street
San Angelo, TX 76903
(915) 658-8009
www.ajra.org

Founded in 1952, this organization is for boys and girls competing in rodeo events. The junior rodeo athletes compete in fourteen events. These events are divided into categories of ages such as eight and under, nine to twelve, thirteen to fifteen, and sixteen to nineteen.

Flying U Rodeo Company
320 Fifth Street
Marysville, CA 95901
(530) 742-8249
www.flyingurodeo.com

This stock contractor describes his "Born to Buck" program, a selective breeding program. At the Flying U Rodeo ranch, two hundred head of bucking horses, one hundred bucking bulls, two hundred steers, one hundred calves, and sixty pick-up horses graze the fields while they await their turn to go to rodeos.

National High School Rodeo Association, Inc. (NHSRA)
12001 Tejon Street, Suite 128
Denver, CO 80234
(800) 466-4772
www.nhsra.org

Descriptions of high school rodeo events, such as bare-back riding, barrel racing, breakaway roping, bull riding, tie-down roping, goat tying, pole bending, queen contest, steer wrestling, saddle bronc riding, and team roping are part of this website. The NHSRA has a membership of more than 12,500 students from the United States, Canada, and Australia, and it sanctions more than 1,100 rodeos each year.

National Intercollegiate Rodeo Association (NIRA)
2316 Eastgate North, Suite 160
Walla Walla, WA 99362
(509) 529-4402
www.collegerodeo.com
The NIRA sponsors scholarships to more than 135 colleges and universities with rodeo organizations on their campus. Members compete in approximately ten rodeos a year trying to earn a trip to the College National Finals Rodeo.

National Little Britches Rodeo Association (NLBRA)
1045 West Rio Grande
Colorado Springs, CO 80906
(800) 763-3694
www.nlbra.com

This association is for kids from ages eight through eighteen who want to experience the sport of rodeo competition. About six hundred members compete in rodeos in eight states.

Professional Rodeo Cowboys Association (PRCA)
101 Pro Rodeo Drive
Colorado Springs, CO 80919
(719) 593-8840
www.prorodeo.com

This website describes the PRCA rodeo events and lists stock of the year and the top fifteen cowboys of the year. An animal welfare booklet can be requested, which describes the care and treatment of professional livestock.

For Further Exploration

Books

Leo Camarillo, *Team Roping*. Colorado Springs, Colorado: Western Horseman, 1982. Describes and shows with many photographs the details of team roping.

Sharon Camarillo, *Barrel Racing*. Colorado Springs, Colorado: Western Horseman, 1985. Demonstrates in photos and text the successful road to barrel racing.

Roy Cooper, *Calf Roping*. Colorado Springs, Colorado: Western Horseman, 1984. With many championships and titles to his name, Cooper tells about calf roping, including throwing the rope, flanking and legging the calf, tying, and rules.

Periodicals

Marilyn Taylor, "Bulldogging School," Arizona Highways, September 1993. Describes the student action at a steer wrestling school.

Michael Parfit, "Rodeos—Behind the Chutes," *National Geographic*, September 1999. Article describes riders' experiences on bareback horses, bulls, saddle broncs, and wrestling with steers as well as other aspects of the rodeo.

Videos

Bull Riders Chasing the Dream. Trinity Films, 1997. This behind-the-scenes look at the dangerous sport of bull riding shows spectacular rides, triumphs, tragedies, injuries, and world champions of the past, present, and future. The video also shows Tuff Hedeman, three-time world champion, on the terrifying bull Bodacious.

Rodeo Gladiator—Eight Seconds to Live or Die! The Broncs Boys; Postproduction: VT-TV, Houston, Texas, 2001. This is the story of Ty Murray, winner of seven All-Around Championships. Shows Murray expertly riding 2,000 pounds of a raging, thrashing bull and tells of Murray's training and struggles.

Index

Picture Credits

About the Author

Judith Janda Presnall is an award-winning nonfiction writer. *Rodeo Animals* is the tenth title in the Animals with Jobs series for KidHaven Press. She has nine other nonfiction titles. Presnall graduated from the University of Wisconsin in Whitewater. She is a member of the Society of Children's Book Writers and Illustrators. Presnall received the Jack London Award for meritorious service in the California Writers Club. She lives in the Los Angeles area with her husband, Lance, and three cats.